# Feathers

Body Coverings

Cassie Mayer

Heinemann Library
Chicago, Illinois

Photo research by Tracy Cummins and Erica Newbery
Designed by Jo Hinton-Malivoire
Printed and bound in China by South China Printing Company
10 09 08 07 06
10 9 8 7 6 5 4 3 2 1

**Library of Congress Cataloging-in-Publication Data**
Mayer, Cassie.
  Feathers / Cassie Mayer.-- 1st ed.
    p. cm. --  (Body coverings)
  Includes bibliographical references and index.
  ISBN 1-4034-8372-8 (hc) -- ISBN 1-4034-8378-7 (pb)
  1. Feathers--Juvenile literature.  I. Title.  II. Series.
  QL697.M43 2006
  598.147--dc22

                                    2005035406

**Acknowledgments**
The author and publisher are grateful to the following for permission to reproduce copyright material:
Corbis pp. **4** (rhino, Royalty Free), **7** and **8** (Theo Allofs), **10** (Tim Davis), **11** and **12** (W. Wisniewski/zefa), **15** (Stuart Westmorland), **16** (Kennan Ward), **20** (Kevin Dodge), **13** and **14** (Michael & Patricia Fogden), **18** (Royalty-Free); Flpa p. **22** (flamingo, L Lee Rue and owl); Getty Images pp. **6** (Campbell), **9** (Van Os); Getty Images/Digital Vision pp. **4** (cheetah), **5**, **23** (kingfisher); Getty Images/PhotoDisc pp. **4** (lizard and snail), **17**, **23** (peacock feathers); Nature Picture Library p. **22** (wood pecker, Dave Watts).

Cover photograph of macaw feathers, reproduced with permission of Gulin/Getty Images. Back cover image of peacock feathers reproduced with permission of Getty Images/PhotoDisc.

Special thanks to the Smithsonian Institution for its help with this project.

Every effort has been made to contact copyright holders of any material reproduced in this book.
Any omissions will be rectified in subsequent printings if notice is given to the publisher.

# Contents

fur

shell

scales

skin

Animals have body coverings.
Body coverings protect animals.

feathers

Feathers are a body covering.
Birds have feathers.

There are different types of feathers.

Feathers can be long.
What bird is this?

This bird is an eagle.
Its feathers help it fly.

Feathers can be short.
What bird is this?

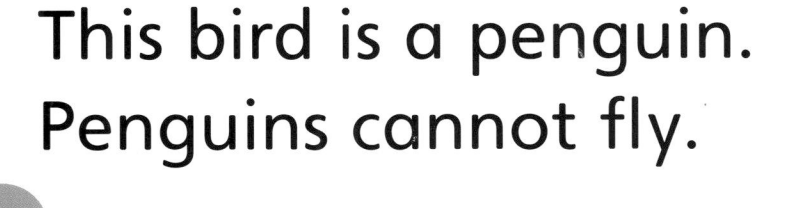

This bird is a penguin.
Penguins cannot fly.

Feathers can be soft.
What bird is this?

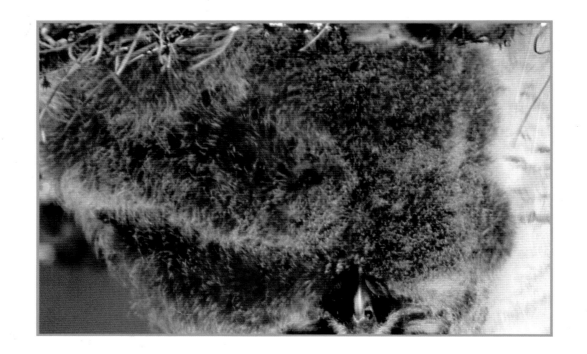

baby snow owl

This bird is a baby snow owl.
Its feathers change as it grows.

Feathers can be stiff.
What bird is this?

This bird is a hummingbird.
It flies in one place like a helicopter.

hover

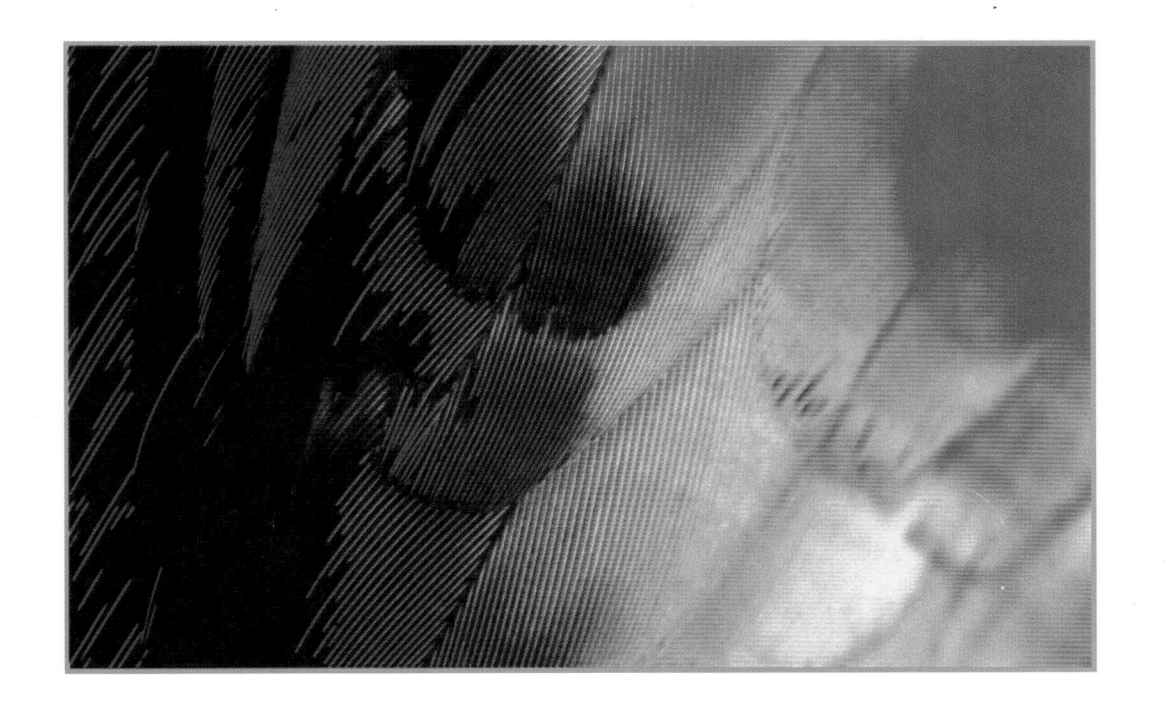

Feathers can be bright colors.
What bird is this?

This bird is a macaw.
Its feathers help it hide.

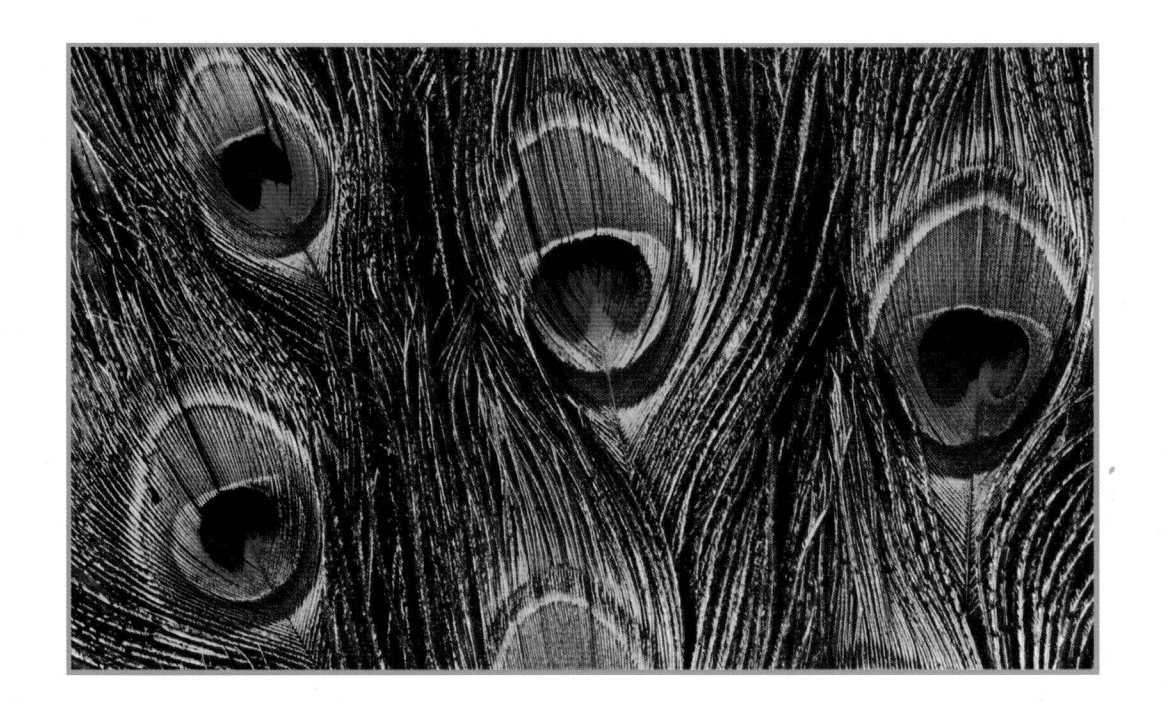

Feathers can have patterns.
What bird is this?

This bird is a peacock.
Its feathers can spread out like a fan.

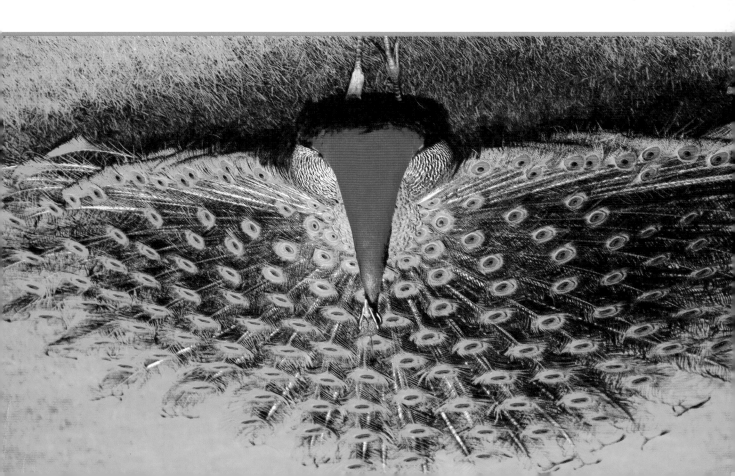

Do you have feathers?

No, you do not have feathers!
You have skin.

What if you had feathers?
What would your feathers be like?

# Fun Feather Facts

Owls have soft feathers that let them fly silently.

Flamingo feathers get their color from the food flamingos eat.

Woodpeckers use their tail feathers to brace against a tree.

# Picture Glossary

**feather** a type of body covering that only birds have

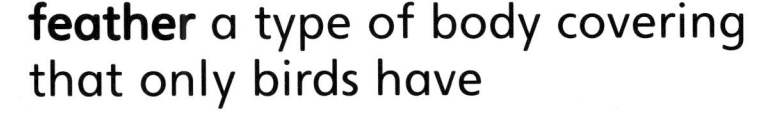

**pattern** a shape or color that repeats over and over again. Patterns help some animals hide.

# Index

**Note to Parents and Teachers**

In this book, children explore characteristics of feathers and are introduced to a variety of animals that use this covering for protection. Visual clues and the repetitive question, "What animal is this?" engage children by providing a predictable structure from which to learn new information. The text has been chosen with the advice of a literacy expert to enable beginning readers success while reading independently or with moderate support. Scientists were consulted to provide both interesting and accurate content.

The book ends with an open-ended question that asks children to relate the material to their lives. Use this question as a writing or discussion prompt to encourage creative thinking and assess comprehension. You can also support children's nonfiction literacy skills by helping them to use the table of contents, picture glossary, and index.